GOING VIRAL

17 Studies to Reach Millions, Gain Influence,

& Achieve Overnight Success

By A.C. Clint

As a show of appreciation to my readers, I've put together FREE resources, including **10 proven techniques to . . .** (1) Build a social following from zero to thousands, (2) create content that audiences are dying to share and (3) Leverage a community of influencers to do word-of-mouth power-lifting for you.

Click HERE, or visit AnnalisC.com to receive FREE resources, including your viral Infographic and cheat sheet.

GOING VIRAL: Reach Millions, Gain Influence, & Learn the Secret to Overnight Success

Chapter 1:
Fifteen Minutes

Grumpy cat. David After the Dentist. Dove's Photoshop Campaign. Sneezing Panda. Dramatic Chipmunk. Diet Coke and Mentos. Chances are, you've *definitely* seen one or all of these memes shared somewhere on your Facebook feed from a friend.

"In the future, everyone will be famous for fifteen minutes" – Andy Warhol

When Andy Warhol said this, I doubt he envisioned a world of Internet, blogging and social media that would make fifteen minutes of fame possible for anyone with the right inspiration and a social media tool box. Entrepreneurs, artists, businesses, creative thinkers, consultants, and aspiring celebrities are in dire need of a medium to rally their fan base and communicate a vision.

“I just put it up on the Internet and it took off,” said no blogger, ever. You might create the most fantastic, life-changing work of art on the planet, but if you don’t tell someone, how will they ever know?

This is why so many incredible artists went to their graves anonymously, only to be discovered by a whirlwind of fame decades later. They were terrible at self-promotion. If you want to enjoy the fruits of your labor in your own lifetime, you’re going to have to get over yourself and share what you do with the world.

Social media places a vast amount of human connections at our fingertips, empowering businesses to capture the attention of the masses and expand connection and influence. But with today’s information overload, the chances of someone visiting a website are slim without the assistance of tactics such as online advertising, content marketing, social media promotion, and search engine optimization.

Customer behavior and spending dollars are migrating online fast, making it increasingly important to drive attention and traffic to your website. Social platforms empower you to broadcast your life, image, and business or product, to an unfathomably large audience. More importantly, digital promotion allows you to empower a niche of loyal and dedicated followers to your brand. Have you ever spent a lot of time and money on a website, creative project, or dream, only to launch to...silence and the chirping of crickets?

With a potential audience of billions and free marketing resources to reach them with, this book is the first place you can look to find out how to align a powerful promotional campaign that will generate profit for a budding business or project.

> "To climb steep hills requires a slow pace at first." William Shakespeare, *Henry VIII.*

Everyone has to start somewhere. Everyone starts at a ground zero Twitter following. The wonderful thing about social media and content marketing that it appreciates over time.

Mainstream media like television and billboards requires a large financial investment up front and produces a flurry of immediate results. Most television and radio commercials are obsolete and forgotten very quickly after launch. Well-conceived blog posts and YouTube videos can live on in infamy by accruing new visitors and customers that may last a lifetime.

Unless you want to be a one-hit wonder, creating content that people love to share and talk about takes patience and skill. Creating viral content calls upon a breadth of resources, skills and talents, and is filled with trial and error experimentation.

Social media is not just binary code, but also a fascinating human behavior study. In the following chapters, I'm going to discuss all of this, and let you in on secret tricks I've discovered in how to light a viral match and pour gasoline to start an unstoppable fire.

Chapter 2:

The Secret to Overnight Success . . .

Viral used to be a bad thing. It meant you had a terrible infectious disease, like the plague. Now, on the brink of a new digital age, the terms have changed. “Going viral” is the elusive brass ring for small businesses, big brands, aspiring celebrities, or any twelve-year-old with YouTube channel dreams of Internet fame.

Viral content is the democracy of media creation. Media from the masses has replaced mass media. Pretty much anything can go viral, if those masses will it, including an article, person, place, video, photo, thought, symbol, hashtag, trend, or tweet.

Viral content at it’s most basic form, is a meme. A meme is "an idea, behavior, or style that spreads from person to person within a culture." Memes are the simplest form of social sharing, and incredibly easy to create.

There are two things that characterize a meme, and its ability to spread like a more fun version of the common cold.

1. Personalization.

A meme occurs when people are motivated to share, by adopting a thought or idea to make it their own. Personalizing an evolving meme typically involves responding with your own inspired version of the original, in the form of parodies, photoshopped images, or GIFs, or any other format you can come up with.

A perfect example of personalization is Nyan Cat, a ten-hour video of a pixelated pop-tart cat flying through outerspace that has over 151 million views. As unexpected as this sensation is, users from around the world began participating by making their own version of Nyan Cat. There is a video for every country from Japan to Bahrain. There is even a dog Nyan Cat.

2. Subcultures.

The meme severely resonates with a small group or subculture, until it reaches what author Malcom Gladwell would call a "tipping point", and explodes into mass appeal. By knowing about it and personalizing it, a meme becomes your own, and in return gives you a sense of belonging to the group or community that also "gets it". This will be explored more in the chapter 'Be Cool'.

'Hipster Little Mermaid' is a perfect meme made to appeal to sub-cultures, by blending tattooed, ironic millennial hipster culture with the stereotypically optimistic Disney princesses of their childhood. Internet-users quickly adopted it by applying their own funny phrases to photos of Ariel in emo glasses. Eventually, fan art turned into Halloween costumes, and avalanched into a cultural sensation.

The viral process really takes flight when users share on sites like Reddit, Twitter, Product Hunt, Facebook and, if it gets really big, eventually jumps over to television networks and news.

This can lead to anything from fifteen seconds to years of Internet fame, until it inevitably fades. Many viral sensations are one-hit wonders that enjoy an explosive rise to the top, only to disappear back into anonymity, or even suffer for years of backlash.

For others, when the Internet Gods smile upon them, they leverage it to build brands, successful entertainment careers, and multi-million dollar businesses that generate success for years to come.

If you intend for your brand or product to become "viral" like those overnight social media phenomena you've heard about, there is a secret to it. The secret is that very few social media success stories actually occur overnight.

Below is an excerpt from *Smartcuts* by Shane Snow, in which he explores the very different fates of two viral stars, and how they were able to leverage their explosion of success.

"In January 2010, Paul 'Bear' Vasquez posted a home video on YouTube. The video idled online for months without attracting any attention, until Jimmy Kimmel discovered the clip in July. He shared it on Twitter and endorsed it as 'the funniest video in the world.' It went viral. Today, 'Double Rainbow' has over 40 million views.

"Around the same time, a 23-year-old Vietnamese American makeup artist named Michelle Phan posted a tutorial on YouTube demonstrating how to apply makeup to recreate Lady Gaga's look from 'Bad Romance.' Buzzfeed picked up the video, and it went viral. Today, it also claims over forty million views.

"Vasquez and Phan took different paths thereafter. Vasquez, who lives just outside of Yosemite National Park in central California, continues to document his life in the mountains, (he has posted over 1,300 clips) but most of his videos only have a few hundred views.

"Phan is the second-most-watched female YouTuber in the world. She claims nearly seven million subscribers and has amassed over one billion views. Thanks to her makeup tutorials, Phan became the official video makeup artist for Lancôme and created her own line for L'Oreal."

Luck and coincidence always plays a factor in success. More importantly, there is a formula to both Michelle Phan's viral tutorial and Double Rainbow guy's success, and I can't wait to show you what it is. I suggest watching both videos online before reading further, available on this companion resource page: http://www.annalisc.com/**viral-resources/**.

Chapter 3:

19 Headline Formulas to Make Your Content Irresistible

So you want to capture someone's attention. The first thing you have to do is find a way to stand out from the noise and clutter. Not an easy feat in the information age. How do you get someone to stop scrolling and start reading and engaging?

You create a hook, something that causes a pause.

Remember a time when you spaced out while skimming an online newsfeed, and without knowing why, found yourself pausing to process the words, or even click? Did you consciously understand why you were clicking? Did you have any control over your finger movement on the mouse? Chances are, like a little fish in the ocean, you encountered a hook.

“5 INSANE PLANS FOR FEEDING WEST BERLIN YOU WON’T BELIEVE ARE REAL.”

“THESE 9 NAZI ATROCITIES WILL MAKE YOU LOSE FAITH IN HUMANITY.”

“6 TITANIC SURVIVORS WHO SHOULD HAVE DIED.”

These are a few titles digital comic strip “XKCD” joked would result if the twentieth century’s most disruptive historical moments occurred in the Internet age.

Click bait headlines aren’t new. The original hook writers were paperboys shouting “Extra! Extra! Read all about it!” headlines on New York streets for Hearst and Pulitzer during the yellow journalism era of the 1920’s.

These days, hook writing is a more subtle art. A hook is usually in the form of an email subject line, a blog title, or a tweet.
The key to writing a hook is opening what I call a ‘curiosity loop’.
That loop can only be closed if a scroller clicks to read more.

A hook or open loop is the first part to evoking the emotion of surprise. It is the joke setup, the building of suspense, the cliffhanger at the end of your favorite Netflix season. If your audience doesn't find out what happens, a gaping question mark will be burned in their psyche forever. It is how J.J. Abrams got so many viewers addicted and frustrated with the television show *Lost*.

Opening a loop is the perfect way to set up a joke or a story. Here are a few subject lines, or tweets, that create a hook with an open loop, or knowledge gap:

"Let me tell you about the weirdest/ scariest/ funniest/ craziest thing that happened to me . . ."

"My 5 favorite tools to beating procrastination . . ."
Why is it that people seem to remember and take notice when you open with an unfinished sentence? It has something to do with our long-term and short-term memory.

I worked my way through college waiting tables. Despite loving food, and getting along great with customers, I had just one problem. I was *terrible* at remembering orders. No matter how hard I listened, my mind would blank on their menu selection the second I left the table.

I recently realized the source of my problem. The explanation was discovered by a Russian psychologist Bluma Zeigarnik years before my failed restaurant career. In 1927, Zeigarnik noticed waiters seemed to remember orders only as long as the order was in the process of being told. Once the order was complete, it became difficult for waiters to recall. What was the reason for this? Short-term memory.

While short-term memories evaporate like rain on a hot sidewalk in summer, long-term memory can store unlimited amounts of information almost indefinitely. The short-term memory gradually transfers important information into long-term memory over time, but only if information is repeated or used. This is why repeated studying helps students perform better on tests.

Your memory's limited capacity can hold about seven items for no more than twenty or thirty seconds at a time. To hold things in short-term memory, we must rehearse them so they don't disappear. This rehearsing takes a lot of brainpower and effort. Zeigarnik realized waiters would juggle open orders in their mind to hold them in short-term memory. Once the order was finished, the waiter could allow the "balls to drop" so to speak.

Zeigarnik Effect = We remember better that which is unfinished or incomplete.

A similar effect also happens over a longer period when we worry about things in our life that have not achieved closure. This is why an unresolved problem at work might haunt you all weekend, or you can never forget that ex who left without explanation.

Storytellers and filmmakers have used the "open loop" for years. This storytelling device is why commercial breaks are tolerated, the culprit for late night *House of Cards* binge watching, and the essential science behind daytime television cliffhanger addiction.

Not only does opening a loop entice a reader, it mentally prepares him or her. Steve Jobs was infamous for doing this in his presentations. He would break down information into pieces (also called chunking), and then prepare the audience for what was to come.

A famous example of this was his opening for his Stanford graduation speech, which he began with, "Today I want to tell you three stories from my life. That's it. No big deal. Just three stories."

Steve Jobs intentionally positioned his products as short "twitter-like headlines", using numbers and analogies to wedge into people's brains. For example:

The iPod: 1000 songs in your pocket.
MacBook Air: The world's thinnest notebook.

Hooks can be used for good or for evil. You may know of sites like Upworthy and Buzzfeed that regularly use hook headlines that have gained a reputation as click bait. If you've ever seen an Upworthy story shared on your Facebook feed, you may recognize this technique at play in the distinctive hyperbolic headlines: "This guy started filming his dog. What happens next will SHOCK you".

When you create a suspenseful hook but don't deliver, your audience will be annoyed and your reputation will quickly be shot. Here are some examples of headlines that over-promise and under-deliver:

"When you read these 19 shocking food facts, you'll never want to eat again."
Payoff: Some foods have a lot of calories.

"You'll NEVER believe what happens when you get 20 Corgi puppies in one room together."
Payoff: Banal video of corgi puppies in a room running around.

This is basically setting up a joke without a punch line by promising the unexpected and delivering the mundane. It is a sure way to get your audience pissed off.

Opening loops is an art of balance. Here is an example of a great open-loop headline:

"What Bruce Lee can teach you about design"

The article delivers on its promise, but doesn't give it all away. If it did, the title would be, "Bruce Lee sets an example that adaptability is the most important quality for a designer to have".

A headline that gives the whole article away is the equivalent of a movie trailer that shows the whole movie in thirty seconds, instead of setting the audience up for an adventure.

Humans love anticipation. Studies show that waiting in line for a product increases the customer's perceived value. Whether it is counting the days until the weekend, buzzing about a new movie coming out, or waiting in line for the next iPhone, using the art of suspense is a sure way to surprise and delight an audience. To help you get started, I've included some open loop prompts to inspire you and get your creative juices flowing when writing your own tweets, headlines, chapter titles, or even pick-up lines.

How to Create an Open Loop:

1. Ask a question
2. Set up an intriguing scenario

3. Create a joke set-up for a punch line

4. Prepare the reader

5. Use a fragment or unfinished sentence

6. Chunk information into numbers

7. Convey desire, story, or conflict (see Storytelling Chapter)

Open Loop Prompts

3 Stories that Illustrate of Power of . . .

This one time I tried . . .

What I learned from . . .

I want to tell you a story about . . .

The craziest/ weirdest/ funniest thing happened to me last week...

How . . . can change your life.

10 Tricks to . . .

5 Tips/ Tools to . . .

The Step-by-Step System to...

The Secret to . . .

How to Become Better at . . .

A brief guide to . . .

Cracking the code to . . .

The surprising formula behind . . .

What you can learn from . . .

How to . . .

The science behind . . .

What . . . says about you.

How to know if . . .

Are you ready to learn my 4-step formula to writing content people love? Or the secret trick Steve Jobs used to add sophistication to presentations? Great. Turn the page.

Chapter 4:

How to Make an 'Information Smoothie'

> "The height of sophistication is simplicity." –
> Clare Boothe Luce

You may have noticed the Top 10 Lists, also known as 'listicles' taking over the Internet in recent years. Why is it that people find top 10 lists so addicting?

Our brains love simplicity. As much as your brain needs learning stimulation, it craves effortlessly acquired information even more.

If you think breaking down your content into numerical items is dumbing your content down, think again. In many ways, organizing your information is the ultimate courtesy to a reader. It is akin to cooking and preparing a meal for someone, instead of throwing raw food on their plate.

One of the masters of communications himself, Steve Jobs perfected the art of organizing and packaging information.

Although he despised bullet points, he was obsessed with the "Power of Three", always breaking his content down into no more than three or four stories or main points.

The numerical list article is inherently captivating for several reasons. To explain to you why our brains are obsessed with numbered lists, I made you (what else?) a numbered list:

1. NUMBERS catch our eye in a content stream.

Numbered lists spatially organize information and promise a story that's finite and easy to read. On a newsfeed, numbers tend to pop among the text and images.

2. CATEGORIES: Numbered lists categorize and chunk information for us.

Your memory's limited capacity can hold about seven items for no more than twenty or thirty seconds at a time. You can trick your short-term memory into holding lots of information by compiling it into chunks.

Chunking is the process of binding individual pieces of information together to make a meaningful whole. For example, you are more likely to remember a phone number broken up as 579 555 6565 (three to seven chunks) than a long string of numbers 5795556565 (one chunk of ten).

Knowing this simple memory trick can change your life, and turn you into a genius mastermind, but I digress.

We can't resist categorizing something the moment we see it, and chunk information into short, distinct components. It is how we make sense of the world. Lists appeal to our tendency — no, our *need* to categorize things.

Chunking is useful when memorizing large amounts of information. By separating individual elements into larger blocks, information becomes easier to retain and recall. Presenting information split into pieces or "chunks" makes reading and understanding faster and easier.

Whether it's because the screen lights are tough on our Internet-addicted eyes, or we all now have the attention span of a fish, chunking is also effective for web reading because readers tend to scan and skip around, rather than read a page sequentially.

3. SPACE: Listicles spatially organize information.

When we process information, we do so spatially. Lists tap into our attention sweet spot. It is our preferred way of receiving and organizing information to guide us with both immediate understanding and later recall.

The Serial Position Effect

The order in which information is presented even impacts our memory and understanding of it. This is known as the "Primacy and Recency Effect". When asked to recall information in list format, the items at the beginning (primacy) and the items at the end (recency) are more likely to be recalled than those in the middle.

There are many ways to beautifully organize your information to make it spatially appealing to the eye:

- Bulleted lists
- Short subheadings
- Short sentences with one or two ideas per sentence
- Short paragraphs (even one sentence)
- Easily scannable text, with bolding of key phrases

- Inline graphics to guide the eyes, or illustrate points which would normally require more words

Infographics

Infographics are those poster-like images that display of data-collections in a beautifully organized visual form. You've probably seen them floating around the web on sites like Pinterest.

These captivating diagrams of numbers, statistics, and icons are perfect for distilling complex information in a playful way that is easy to consume and share.

Not long ago, you would need to hire an illustrator or designer to help you create one of these files or images. But, thanks to sites like Canva, you can easily create your own collection of ideas and data. Aside from promoting your creation on social media, there are many excellent sites devoted to infographics that would get you extra sharing traction.

- Daily Infographic
- Cool Infographics
- Infographics Archive

- Infographic Journal
- Infographics Showcase

4. TIME: Listicles promise a story that's finite, meaning the length has been quantified upfront.

In an age of information overload, our time and attention is precious to us. In fact, our mental health and sanity is beginning to depend on it. The "paradox of choice" is the theoretical phenomenon that stems from the rainbow of choices capitalism has thrust upon the average consumer.

Although being spoiled for choice encourages us to spend and purchase more, the extra effort to decide comes with fatigue, regret, self-blame, analysis paralysis, and opportunity costs.

In short, the more we have to choose from, the worse we feel. More information and options leads to questioning ourselves and being fully aware that we are always "missing out" on other options. There is even an Internet meme hashtag created for this, know as #FOMO (fear of missing out).

While many choices may increase our desire to consume, it also decreases our satisfaction levels and drains our willpower and mental decision making abilities.

In 2011, psychologists Claude Messner and Michaela Wänke investigated how to alleviate the depression of information overwhelm thrust upon us by modern times. They concluded that reducing the amount of conscious work we have to do to process information causes us to make decisions faster, and become happier.

The numbered article is irresistible because it promises a definite ending. We then are rewarded with a reinforcing and illusory sense of accomplishment. We have completed something for the day, even if it was just reading a click bait article.

Is reading dead? I hope the Internet hasn't killed our ability to consume in-depth information and think critically. I myself am reading more books than ever thanks to audio book apps. Whether you are looking to pen the next *War and Peace*, or drive traffic to your website, presenting your argument, sales pitch, or perspective in a way that many people will understand, and be inclined to consume, is the ultimate superpower.

Information Smoothie Action Steps:

1. Brainstorm and write your content.
2. Consider how you can break it down into numbers or bullet points. The "10 Things I Learned . . ." template is a fantastic way to get your brain rolling on content generation.
3. Format for screen reading. Use paragraphs, line spaces, bold, italic, numbers, hyperlinks, and underlining to emphasize key points, and make them pop among blocks of text.

Next up, I'm going share five of my craziest secrets you *need* to know about if you want to be a viral success. *Sneak Peek*: you'll learn why people are obsessed with Jennifer Aniston's face, our funny biological response to naked photos, and how emojis are changing your brain.

Chapter 5:

The 5-Step Formula for Telling a Fantastic Story

Whether it's a “Breaking Bad” binge, a Jane Austen remake, or a pal telling us about the *crazy* night they had at the bar on Saturday, everyone loves a good story.

Stories teach and persuade effectively.

Have you ever had to sit through a boring PowerPoint presentation in a class or a meeting? It can be rough trying to hold focus.

When someone relays a dry piece of information to you, it activates only one part of your brain called the “Broca's area and Wernicke's area”. This is the part of the brain we use to decode words into meaning. And that's it. Nothing else happens.

When we are told a story, something completely different occurs: our entire brain begins to light up like fireworks. The Broca's area and Wernicke's area activates to decipher the text, but then more brain regions perk up as well, vicariously experiencing the story we are being told.

Plain old text only activates the word-processing part of our brain. However, sensory words elicit responses that cause us to be more emotionally and physically involved in what we are listening to or reading.

In a 2006 study published in the NeuroImage journal, researchers in Spain asked participants to read words with strong odor associations, while scanning their brains with an MRI machine. When reading words associated with inanimate objects like "chair" and "key", the sensory cortex remained dark. However, when subjects looked at Spanish words associated with strong-smelling things like "perfume" and "coffee", the part of the brain that recognizes smell (primary olfactory cortex) completely lit up. When I describe a buttery, lobster dinner I ate last night, your sensory cortex lights up. If I tell a story about running from a thief, your motor cortex gets going and you start running along with me. This makes storytelling elements such as metaphors and descriptive words all the more powerful.

"Metaphors like 'The singer had a velvet voice' and 'He had leathery hands' roused the sensory cortex. [...] Then, the brains of participants were scanned as they read sentences like "John grasped the object" and "Pablo kicked the ball." The scans revealed activity in the motor cortex, which coordinates the body's movements." - Annie Murphy Paul, "Your Brain on Fiction", **The New York Times**, 2012.

Because our imagination is so strong, listening to a well-written story is almost as good as experiencing it in real life.
Because certain words and storytelling techniques activate sensory regions of the brain, listening to well told stories can cause an audience's neural and brain behavior to mimic that of a speaker.

According to Uri Hasson from Princeton, telling stories that have really impacted one's life can spark a listener's interest so profoundly that the two brains begin to actually sync:

"When the woman spoke English, the volunteers understood her story, and their brains synchronized. When she had activity in her insula, an emotional brain region, the listeners did too. When her frontal cortex lit up, so did theirs. By simply telling a story, the woman could plant ideas, thoughts and emotions into the listeners' brains."

The powerful art of storytelling can allow others to experience things the same way you have experienced them, by activating their brain in the same way your brain has been activated.

Is storytelling the literal ability to control other people's brains? It's a scary thought, but also an exciting one. We can weave magical spells around us with the right combination of words.

How can you tell a story that will illuminate all of the dendrites in your audience's brain? Storytelling is easier than you think. The brain automatically seeks out patterns and anomalies to help us make sense of the world. This is why we find faces in clouds, songs in sound beats, and story patterns in information.
The ancient language of storytelling has helped our brain make sense of the world for as long as words have been strewn together into sentences. Our impulse to detect story patterns is so powerful that we can find them even when they're not there.

I even have a story about that: In 1944, Fritz Heider & Marianne Simmel held the landmark study 'An Experimental Study of Apparent Behavior' in which thirty-four Massachusetts college students were shown a short film featuring two triangles and a circle moving across a two-dimensional surface.

When asked what had happened in the film, the students imagined elaborate narratives and vivid emotional motives. A common plot theme detected among the shapes included interpreting the triangles as two men fighting, and the circle as a woman trying to escape the bullying triangle. The subjects attached emotions such as fear or anger to the geometric shapes.

Only one test subject saw this scene for what it was: geometric shapes moving across a screen. *That* is how easy it is to tell a story. Humans can anthropomorphize almost anything without dialogue, music, or even structure.

To be a really potent communication form, stories will typically draw upon devices like archetypes and plot structure to keep us engaged and involved. I'm going to share a few story formulas with you that will make your next email, conversation, keynote presentation, or viral video explode with success.

My special story-telling formula is based on an element of the human condition that will resonate with nearly everyone: DESIRE. DESIRE is what drives us, plagues us, brings joy, and motivates us to reach new heights and depths of the human experience. There are entire religions based upon eliminating it from your life, with the ironic twist that the need to eliminate desire is a desire within itself.

To put desire into a formula, writers, actors, and storytellers use something called beats. Without diving too deeply into Screenwriting 101, beats are small desires characters have through a story that gets them from one moment to the next. They are small or large desires that drive behavior.

Longer stories, like movies and television series, are broken up into a series of "beats", represented by moments in which characters take actions to get where he or she wants.
A story almost always features a hero or protagonist who wants something and is going after it. They either get it, or don't get it, but catharsis occurs in an audience if the hero ultimately learns something from their experience.

How to tell a great story:

1. Think of a hero (it can be yourself or someone you know, or you can just make one up).

Example: Let's say you are the hero.

2. Give the hero a desire.

Example: As the hero, you wake up one morning. You are hungry and want a banana.

3. Put an obstacle (or several) in the way of the hero.

Example: You check the fridge, and the banana is gone. Did your roommate eat the last banana?

4. Make the hero try to solve or overcome the obstacle.

Example: You go to the grocery store, and they are out of bananas. You write an angry letter to all of your roommates, trying to figure out who ate the banana. When no one comes clean, you try to uncover hidden clues as to who ate the banana. You are the now Nancy Drew in the "Mystery of the Missing Banana", interrogating suspects and getting your hands dirty.

5. The hero either solves it or doesn't solve it, *but learns something in the process.* A hero's growth is a critical component to a reader's catharsis effect.

Example: After berating your roommates over email, a memory flashback reveals you actually ate the banana and forgot about it. You might not have your banana, but you've learned it is silly to blame other people for your overzealous appetite and memory gaps. You buy everyone a bushel of bananas, laugh it off, and grow as a person.

Ultimately, creating a killer story is all about highlighting a struggle or conflict. This struggle is often in the form of the antagonist. In the banana story, the antagonist is a roommate (we think). But, in a surprise twist, the antagonist is the hero herself. This is what makes stories a really addicting socially acceptable drug, and what drives the multi-billion dollar entertainment industry.

Stories don't have to be complicated to be engaging. Often stories feature a beginning, middle, and typically end in a resolution. It is all the more effective if there is a protagonist who wants something, and finds a way to get it in the end.

Wanting something and facing obstacles towards getting it creates conflict, and conflict creates suspense. The longer and more complex it is for the story's hero to succeed, the more invested we become. The protagonist can be working towards a bigger goal, or something small.

Loglines, Elevator Pitches, Headlines, and Tweets

Every story, sitcom, movie, viral video, or novel can be distilled into what is known in the film biz as a "logline". Viral sensations also have their own logline in the form of an abbreviated tweet, meme, or headline that typically goes viral.

Viral Video Producer Karen X has skyrocketed to viral fame a couple of times, in large part because of her ability to churn out brilliant one-line hooks for her three-minute viral stories.

Her viral video "Girl Learns to Dance in a Year (TIME LAPSE)" has over six million views, in part because she is able to highlight desire and conflict in a simple video headline: Girl (the hero) wants to dance, and perseveres with practice to accomplish her goal in a year.

Both of these headlines pack a viral punch using numbers, desire, conflict, and accomplishment, along with the promise of awe and the unexpected.

Story is first a formula, and second, a beautiful reflection of the human condition. We all find meaning in our lives by overcoming obstacles and learning lessons. Watching and listening to stories is a way for us to take part in the profound experience, often in ninety minutes or less.

We don't actually have to get off our couch to embark on an epic journey through the underworld, or battle good versus evil, and maybe even earn a takeaway experience or lesson.

When communicating about your professional brand or personal life, consider if there is a possible story behind it. And if so, how will you tell it?

Now that you know the basic story structure and formula, let's find out how we can paint the color of this framework with emotion in chapter six. . .

Chapter 6:

Three Viral Emotions that Get Shared the Most

Sharing online content, whether an interesting article or a funny YouTube clip, has become an integral part of the modern human experience.

People are most likely to share subject matter that evokes a deep emotion in them, whether it is pride, joy, disbelief, humor, disappointment, or excitement. Some emotions spread faster than others, but any sort of emotional impact goes a long way.

I put this emotional principle to practice during my time for a non-profit company. With a limited budget, we had no choice but to bootstrap to create awareness for a brand or product. We looked for a compelling story and we found one: a blind client of ours who enjoyed backpacking in his spare time named Marc.

Marc had an obstacle: he wanted to go rock-climbing and camping, but lacked the resource of vision. Through evoking the powers of his other four senses, and his personal passion within, he overcame this obstacle to pursue his sense of adventure and do what he loves.

Many people lack the bravery or motivation to camp in the wilderness or climb dangerous heights, even with full eyesight. Marc's story is one of empowerment and perseverance, which would inspire awe in anyone, which is exactly what I was going for.

1. Awe

Now is a great time to give the "Double Rainbow" video another watch, to understand why it resonates with over four million people and counting.

The rainbow in this video is a breath-taking natural phenomenon, of course, but even more fascinating is the extreme rainbow of emotion the narrator experiences. He tastes every color from to awe and surprise, to tears of joy.

A double rainbow would inspire awe in anyone, but when his emotion is experienced in nearly hyperbolic excess, surprise and humor ensues, catapulting the virality of the video to the next level.

In his book, *Contagious: Why Things Catch On*, Jonah Berger examines why science articles tend to spread rapidly, citing the reason that they "frequently chronicle innovations and discoveries" that evoke a feeling of awe in readers.

Of all the emotional content shared on the Internet, the feeling that spreads the fastest and the farthest is awe: that sense of excitement and wonderment from encountering great beauty, knowledge, or human accomplishment.

2. Anger (Fear in Disguise)

Anger and fear are two emotions that go hand in hand. Anger is usually the result of someone feeling threatened. Either their worldview is being encroached upon, or they are fearful for themselves or others.

Fear triggers anger, which triggers a biological “fight or flight” response. The chances that content will get shared depends on how "activated" a person feels after encountering it. While sadness causes people to withdraw, anger triggers a biological “fight or flight” response, making it a powerful emotion that incites us to take action.

Sina Weibo is a Chinese micro-blogging site similar to Twitter. Researchers used this platform to track "emoji" emotions of millions of messages posted. Their finding uncovered that joy spreads quicker than sadness or disgust, but nothing speeds through the Internet quite as rapidly as *rage*.

If you have ever been on the receiving end of a social media damage control situation, this will come as no surprise to you. When outrage strikes, it hits fast and goes far, leaving total wreckage in its wake.

In his book *Trust Me, I'm Lying*, Ryan Holiday discusses how PR reps and marketers can leverage outrage to pit media outlets and groups against each other to gain mass exposure, nearly for free. Working on a shoestring budget, Holiday was tasked with publicity for famed misogynist "bro" Tucker Max's book-to-film premiere of *I Hope They Serve Beer in Hell*. To pull it off, he used the power of rage to stage an epic saga, pitting Tucker Max against feminist publication *Jezebel*.

Holiday defaced billboard ads that he himself had placed, with protest stickers he made. He then sent photos of the vandalism to blogs claiming it was part of a real protest movement against Max's sexism. This inevitably spawned an outcry and avalanche of media attention for the film.

Is all press good press? If you look to stir the sleeping beast of Internet anger, approach with caution. Being on the receiving end of an internet-troll stoning can damage an online brand that no amount of SEO or press spin can save.

3. Surprise and Humor

Magic and comedy have something in common. If you have ever had secret dreams of being a standup comic, here is a cool secret to get your career started.

The number one element that triggers human laughter is *surprise*. In comedy, surprise is like a verbal magic trick. If you think of a magic act, a magician surprises the audience when he does his trick. If there is no surprise, there is no trick. Without formulating surprise, you're going to have one hell of a boring act.

How is surprise created? The easiest way is to lead the audience to assume one thing and then produce the opposite. That's why they call it a punchline. It punches you with unexpectedness. It confuses our brain, and we don't know how to react, so we giggle like a newborn baby experiencing something unexpected for the first time again.

Set Up: *I woke up in the hotel this morning and the housekeeper was banging on the door, just banging!*
Punch: *...Finally, I had to get up and let her out.*

The joke produces the assumption of a common situation. Most people have been in a hotel room and disturbed by a knocking housekeeper. To everyone's surprise, she is trapped in the room, trying to get out. This is called a "reverse" in comedy.

Of course, master of performance, Steve Jobs, always carried these types of surprises up his sleeve. When Jobs first told the audience that Apple was going to introduce a mobile phone, he said, "Here it is." Instead of showing the iPhone, the slide displayed a photo of an iPod with an old-fashioned rotary dial, to the audience's delight and amusement.

Set-Up: Audiences expects new, cutting-edge technology

Punch line: Instead, an antiquated, abandoned technology is produced.

This is why bad click bait is doomed to fail. It promises a punch (surprise) but doesn't deliver.

Create an inside joke.

Have you watched the American comedy series *The Office*? If so, you're familiar with office prankster Jim Halpert, and his hopeless victim Dwight Schrute. Jim is quintessential cool, and poor Dwight is like the little brother that everyone can't help but pick on. Most of the episodes play out a brotherly dynamic between Jim terrorizing Dwight with silly office pranks. Jim stays calm and smirks knowingly at the camera, while Dwight takes everything very seriously, and gets easily flustered and upset. For years, this sitcom managed to create an inside joke with a nationwide audience of viewers.

Creating an inside joke is a literary technique known as dramatic irony. **Dramatic irony** occurs when the audience has all the inside information, while the story protagonist or character has no idea what's going on. This produces a dramatic, and often funny, conflict.

Dramatic irony has three stages—installation, exploitation, and resolution, also sometimes called preparation, suspension, and resolution. The audience knows something one or more of the characters don't, which creates the perfect inside joke.

The Office is filled with dramatic irony. Jim and the audience know what pranks being pulled, while Dwight remains clueless and frustrated.

HBO's *West World* creates tremendous dramatic irony as robots discover they are not human and rekindle their real identities, circuitry, and past identities. The 90's classic *Mrs. Doubtfire* creates dramatic irony as Robin Williams nannies in drag, and only the audience knows his secret. In *The Truman Show*, the audience, director, and *entire world* know Truman is playing the television character of himself, while Truman does not. Watching him discover it for himself creates an intensely dramatic conflict.

Look closely and you will find dramatic irony everywhere. All of these plot lines are fascinating and compelling because of an "us" versus "them": an inside joke.

There are many different types of irony that can help you create surprise and humor:

- Verbal Irony (sarcasm)
- Situational irony (you try for one thing, but get something completely different)
- Cosmic irony (the Gods are playing with you)
- Historical Irony (Titanic, the ship that couldn't sink, sunk)

Parody is another method to get your audience laughing and sharing your stuff. A parody (also know as spoof, send-up, take-off, or lampoon) is a work created to imitate, make fun of, or comment on an original work by means of satiric or ironic imitation. When a cultural formula grows old or overdone, it is usually subject to parody. If you would like to use parody to add humor to your viral story, here are a few action steps:

Action Steps and Formulas to Evoke Emotion

Parody

1. Find a pop culture reference
2. Find a subculture
3. Exaggerate subculture to the absurd/hyperbole
4. Add in multiple references
5. Have a straight man so there is recognition of the parody nature

Surprise

1. Setup up an ordinary expectation.
2. Surprise with something different (punchline).

Awe

Inspire the emotion of awe with science articles, beautiful landscapes, physical feats, and anything impressive or out of the ordinary.

***Rage:**

Find two passionate groups or subcultures, and pit them against each other (bros and feminists, democrats and republicans). Use snarky copy-writing tone to call out specific people.

**Inciting rage is low-hanging fruit, and not always recommended for your professional brand or personal reputation.*

Chapter 7:

Show and Tell: The Picture Superiority Effect

Do me a favor and blink your eyes. See how long that took? Recent studies from MIT suggest that it takes one tenth the blink of an eye (thirteen milliseconds) for us to process an image, and another one hundred milliseconds for us to attach meaning to it. Just one blink is how long it takes for your brain to recognize and register a visual cue. This is why humans are visual creatures above all else. Reading has only been around for a few thousand years, but we have been using images to communicate since our evolution began.

Maybe it's a cliché, but only because it is true: a picture speaks a thousand words. When it comes to retaining certain types of information, text and oral presentations get completely demolished.

The Picture Superiority Effect describes the phenomenon that images are more likely to be remembered than words. Words can take up to twice as long to process than photos. If information is spoken, people remember about ten percent of it seventy-two hours later. The ability to recall information increases to a whopping sixty-five percent when pictures are added.

Repeated testing has shown that people can encounter a sequence of photos for under ten seconds and still remember more than 2,500 pictures with at least ninety percent accuracy. Photo recall accuracy reduces to just under sixty-three percent several days later, and can still be reliably retrieved several decades later from test participants.

What is our aversion to text? As brain scientist John Medina puts it, wordy text literally "chokes your brain", even for the fastest speed-reader. This is because the brain sees words as long sequences of many tiny pictures strewn together that must be deciphered individually.

This explains why hieroglyphs were the original alphabet, the appeal of Japanese symbols as tattoos, and why emojis have taken flight as our new emotional alphabet. It also explains why you couldn't help spacing out during your co-worker's bullet-point-laden PowerPoint presentation the other week.

Your Brain on Vision

Two-thirds of your brain is dedicated to the functioning of your vision. While twenty percent manages "visual-only" functioning, the other forty percent is involved in our vision's relationship with touch, motor skills, attention, spatial navigation, or meaning. This explains why Trend Reports indicate that sixty-five to eighty-five percent of people describe themselves as visual learners, and why videos and photos tend to catch viral fire more rapidly than text-only tweets and blog posts.

Our connection to images is more innate and emotional, which prompts us to take action more quickly. Because our color and image perceptions function so quickly, visual cues cause us to engage or disengage, before even consciously realizing our decision.

There are numbers to prove it. Here are a few statistics indicating why photos are powerful drivers of viral social content:

- Photos receive the highest interaction from Facebook users and photos can boost retweets by thirty-five percent.

- Photos accounted for seventy-five percent of content posted by Facebook pages worldwide.

- Photos are the most engaging type of content on Facebook with a whopping eighty-seven percent interaction rate.

No other post type received more than a four percent interaction rate.

- Photos get fifty-three percent more likes than other posts. Users are also more likely to engage with brands that post photos over those who do not.

- Adding a photo URL to your tweet can boost retweets by an impressive thirty-five percent, according to research by Media Blog's content analysis of over two million tweets sent by thousands of users over the course of a month.

You get it. We love to look at pictures. But what do we love to look at the most? To find out, keep reading.

Chapter 8:

The Jennifer Aniston Brain Cell

Friends sitcom star Jennifer Aniston is well known in the magazine business as a cover performance darling.

Putting her as the cover girl is proven to sell more copies, which is probably why her love life scandals have been played out exhaustively in the media. No one can deny that there is just something about Aniston that people can't get enough of.

Jennifer Aniston's face also contributed to a profound breakthrough in our understanding of the neurological response to familiar faces. For social survival, our brain has developed a specific circuit for recognizing faces called the "fusiform gyrus".

From the moment we are born, facial recognition becomes an integral part in our visual understanding of the world. This is important from an evolutionary perspective. The ability to differentiate from the pack leader, your sister, and your mate of choice is essential to survival and healthy procreation. We are not alone in the ability to recognize faces. Even monkeys and sheep (the animal that epitomizes sameness to us) are unique to one another.

In 2005, researchers led by Dr. Christof Koch at Caltech inserted electrodes into the brains of patients with epilepsy to record the seizure activity to better understand our facial recognition circuitry.

These researchers showed patients a series of faces, including famous celebrities, close friends and family, and random strangers (for control purposes). The electrodes in the fusiform gyrus recorded the neural activity for these faces, and revealed that cells responded to each face in a specifically different way.

In one patient, there was what is now known as "the Jennifer Aniston cell". This neuron fired only when the patient was shown a picture of Jennifer Aniston. Nothing else was able to elicit a response. The neuron was only activated by Aniston's face.

This goes to show the power of a recognizable face, and what it does to our brains. No wonder a website called "Facebook" (a literal web "book" of familiar faces) exploded into global mass appeal. Faces, especially recognizable ones, instinctually urge us to click, share, and engage.

Chapter 9:

The Trick Disney, Cereal Boxes, and Italian Courtiers Use to Create an Unspoken Connection

“You have really beautiful . . .eyes” might be a cheesy pick-up line but it may be more truthful than it seems.

Did you know first dates are more likely to result in a love match if the pair gazes into each other’s eyes for a minute or longer?

Humans love the feeling of connection that comes from gaze and eye contact.

Eye maps have shown us that when we encounter photos of other people, we look to the eyes first in an effort to connect. That means if their eyes are pointed somewhere else, we tend to follow.

Humans instinctively want to look at each other, or what someone else is looking at. If you want to test this theory for yourself, you can perform your own gaze experiment. Stand on a street corner and look up in amazement or confusion. Typically, multiple bystanders will start looking up with you.

This non-verbal trick also works in advertising. Funny but disturbing proof of the eye contact connection becomes evident in the infamous cereal box eye-gaze trick.

Visit any grocery store and notice where the characters on the cereal boxes cartoon characters are looking. At first glance, you might infer they are gazing at a scrumptious bowl of cereal.

Look again, and remember that the target market for sugary cereal is the younger, more vertically impaired segment of the population. Yes, cereal box cartoons are designed to make eye contact with children.

The Food and Brand Lab tested this theory by showing subjects cereal boxes with Trix the Rabbit making eye contact or not making eye contact. The study revealed that when the silly Trix Rabbit and Tony the Tiger made eye contact with customers, brand trust increased sixteen percent, and a feeling of connection increased twenty-eight percent. Participants also just "liked Trix better" when eye contact was made.

So Trix really are for kids, and for cereal box designers.

If you want to apply this trick to enhance your digital brand, try directing a model's gaze towards a call to action, like a button or sign-up form, will cause the viewer to also focus on that action point.

In 1872, Charles Darwin discovered that the sensation of fear caused our pupils to expand as a survival instinct. Pupils expand to let light in, and the more we can see, the more chances we have to survive. Our pupils also expand when we see something we like and want to take in more of.

In 1965, a psychologist named Eckhard Hess built upon this theory with his assistant, James Polt. As an experiment, he showed multiple photographs while tracking the diameter of Polt's pupil size. Of all of the photos, one in particular caused Polt's pupils to grow round and black.

What photo contents that had this crazy effect? A naked woman.

As a positive feedback loop, humans also find dilated pupils attractive. Eyes become all the more potent as a visual cue when pupils are dilated.

Italian courtiers in the 16th century may have discovered this before James Polt. Realizing dilated pupils gave them a more seductive look; courtiers would take eye drops laced with the toxic herb Belladonna to keep their pupils from constricting.

Evidence of our attraction to dilated pupils really comes to life when you experiment with pupil size testing on the opposite sex. In one study, two groups of men were gathered and shown photos of women.

A control group was shown original photos, while the experiment group saw images of faces with pupils modified to look darker and larger. The exact same faces were consistently rated as more attractive with larger pupils.

Have you ever noticed the enormous eye span of popular cartoon characters like Mickey the Mouse and the Little Mermaid? Disney animates everything from princesses to Pixar characters with larger-than-life pupils, which gives audiences a deeper sense of connection to the characters.

This explains why cats and babies keep blowing up the Internet. Big eyes are a neonatal feature that triggers our innate biological nurturing instinct. Humans are hard-wired to respond to the evolutionary allure of large forehead and eyes, chubby cheeks, small chin, and soft frame because of its nurturing association with babies and offspring.

When we see something “cute”, it even stimulates our mesocorticolimbic system, the part of the brain associated with the processes of motivation, and causes a surge of the feel-good neurotransmitter, dopamine. Yes- looking at cute photos is in fact, a bit of a legal high.

Remember Michelle Phan, who skyrocketed to makeup tutorial fame? She posted over fifty how-to videos on YouTube before her Lady GaGa video went viral.

Of all the high-quality videos she posted, why did just one strike it rich? Was it luck? Coincidence? Or is there a subtle psychological cue that attracted millions to watch?

If you navigate to Phan's YouTube page and scroll, it will quickly become clear why this video stood out to viewers, again and again.

Whether intentional or inadvertent, it is impossible not to be grabbed by the arrestingly large "googley eyes" featured in the video preview. The tutorial itself is a modern-day, digital belladonna tincture that will teach you how to expand your pupils with makeup and computer generation tricks, to achieve the look of enormous anime pupils.

Chapter 10:

How Emojis Are Changing Your Brain ☺

Facial expressions are a universal communication that transcends culture, race, class, and time. From the second we meet someone, we begin spending a great deal of visual effort attempting to decode the micro-expressions on their face.

If you closely watch someone speak, you will notice that body language and facial expressions are often far more revealing than the words coming out of their mouth.

If you were suddenly transported five hundred years into the past, or to a remote jungle-dwelling tribe, you would still be able to use the power of facial expressions to navigate your new social surroundings, despite seemingly insurmountable cultural and language differences.

Aside from pleasing the eye, you can also use facial expressions to signal action.

The Facial Feedback Hypothesis

Have you ever been having a bad day and some stranger tells you to smile? Irritating perhaps, but there is some science to your ability to change your mood with a facial expression. The Facial

Feedback Hypothesis asserts that when we make a face, it causes us to feel the matching emotion.

Primates like us have these cool things in our brains called "mirror neurons". These neurons encourage us to mimic or mirror the person we are looking at. Mirror neurons fire both when an animal acts, and when the animal observes another performing an action. The neuron mirrors the behavior of another, as though the observer were acting.

Mirroring others is an important and fantastic way to learn new things, connect with someone via body language, and feel empathy for others. You can also use mirror neurons to visually communicate to an audience.

For example, if we see a confused or unhappy face on a website, we tend to copy the face, and feel more confused or unhappy ourselves. If we see a smiling face in our newsfeed, we will also feel a touch of levity.

The Power of Emoji Communication

Walk down the aisles of Walmart, and you'll find it impossible to ignore the latest emoji trend hitting the aisles. They are everywhere. Emoji pillows, emoji wrapping paper, emoji masks. Without this special smiling face symbol, our chats and emails would be devoid of humor, sarcasm, and the occasional flirtation.

The "smiley face" has permeated pop culture for decades now, reinventing itself more times than Madonna. It went viral before "viral" was even a thing.

Here is why: as a species, we are delighted by euphoric facial expressions. Our desire to recognize faces and emotion runs so deep, that we even anthropomorphize simple punctuation marks. And this new keyboard language style appears to actually be morphing our brain.

According to a study published in the journal *Social Neuroscience*, the parentheses and colon "happy face" now activates the occipitotemporal parts of the brain, triggering the same facial recognition response that occurs when we encounter human faces.

According to researcher Owen Churches of Flinders University, Australia:

“There is no innate neural response to emoticons that babies are born with. Before 1982 there would be no reason that ‘:-)’ would activate face sensitive areas of the cortex. Now it does because we’ve learnt that this represents a face . . .This is an entirely culturally created neural response. It’s really quite amazing.”

The response to :) is learned, not innate. While the :) and :-) are now being processed as actual faces, the non-standard (-: does nothing for us.

Before we scoff at millennial dependency on emoji communication in lieu of loquacious SAT verbiage, consider how these pithy symbols can activate facial recognition and mirror neurons in the brains of your audience. The ability to persuade with primal expressions, as well as words, is a super tool you will want to have in your persuasion box.

Chapter 11:

Mesmerizing with Motion

Have you ever seen the way a cat gravitates to a piece of bouncing string? The cat could probably care less when the same string is inanimate. However, when the string moves, something in the cat's brain signals excitement and interest. This is because cats are designed to be the ultimate predators. Catching moving things is their meal ticket.

Just like cats, our ability to detect motion is a biological instinct once imperative to hunting and threat detection. To ensure survival, you have two types of cells in your eyes: rods and cones. Cones are in the middle, and used for seeing detail and color. Rods see only black and white, but are fantastic at detecting low light levels, movement, and small changes in our peripheral vision.

Rods once were used to alarm us to sabre-tooth cats about to pounce. Now they are more useful in alerting a dodgeball about to hit us on the head, or a car threatening to run us over.

Our motion sensors also keep our brain alert and interested in what it is seeing. This is why movement captures attention, and the imagination.

Our gravitational pull to moving things might explain why videos are the exploding in social media right now. If a picture paints a thousand words, then one minute of video is worth 1.8 million, according to Forrester's researchers.

According to a Socialbakers study, video posts have the most organic reach of any type of Facebook post. Facebook is even starting to eclipse YouTube with its video uploads and viral shares and comments.

An influx of new social sites are sensing this trend and capitalizing on it, including SnapChat's video posting tool, Periscope's live streaming capabilities, and of course the grandmother of viral video-sharing, YouTube. Facebook and Twitter even use an automatic play feature that causes videos to take motion and start as a user scrolls through their social feed.

GIFS

Our fascination with movement also explains the latest GIF addiction sweeping the Internet. GIFs (short for Graphics Interchange Format) refer to a type of file that is essentially an animated, moving photo.

GIFs are attention grabbing because they are simpler and easier to watch than videos. They mesmerize with looping motion, and are able to pack an information punch with visuals and captions. They are silent, consume less time, and can more quickly and efficiently communicate a concept while retaining the visually catching animation of a video.

In every way GIFs are primed to be the perfect viral storm. Often in the meme sharing process, viral videos will be quickly turned into GIFs so they can be broken down and easily viewed on Tumblr and other social sharing sites. Bonus points are that you can watch them silently at work, without the sound accidentally turning on and giving you away to your boss.

GIFs can make an email marketing piece more entertaining, enhance instructional blogs, highlight a call-to-action, or rapidly increase a video's viral punch by quickly distilling main points.

Chubbies Shorts Weekenders edition email marketing blast (http://www.chubbiesshorts.com/pages/the-weekend-has-arrived) features GIF memes and customer Instagram posts that are entertaining and primed for sharing. LiveStrong is another brand that regularly utilizes the GIF to quickly and easily illustrate exercise movements on their blogs and marketing pieces.

Action Steps:

Thanks to cell phones, creating a shareable video is already at your fingertips, and GIPHY.com and other websites supply simple tools to easily convert video into GIF format. A quick Google search will pop up multiple GIF-making tools that will allow you to string together several images into an animated slideshow.

If you would like to find out how to creatively implement GIFs into your brand, check out my YouTube tutorial here: https://www.youtube.com/watch?v=NO559fCLvSc

Chapter 12:

Names, Names, Names: Influencer Priming

> "Remember that a person's name is, to that person, the sweetest and most important sound in any language"
> - Dale Carnegie, *How to Win Friends and Influence People.*

Have you ever met someone at a cocktail party, been introduced, and several moments later blanked on their name? Painful for everyone, right?

I have a friend who met the President of the United States. Every time I hear a story about someone meeting a presidential candidate, it goes something like this:

"Yeah, y'know, at first I wasn't that into his campaign, but we were introduced and he shook my hand. We talked a little bit and it was really cool, and then later, right before he left, he said good-bye and *remembered my name."*

What followed was a lot of praise about the presidential candidate from my friend, who one had been on the fence about their vote, and was now a total convert.

Our names are a big deal to us. This is bad news for me. I am terrible at recalling names. Thankfully Facebook provides me with digital flashcards for all my friends and relatives. When I meet someone new, I immediately add him or her as a connection on Twitter or LinkedIn, in hopes of burning his or her name into my brain forever. Or, at least for an hour.

There are lots of studies that validate the importance of name recall as an innate social grace. The study "What's in a Name? A Complementary Means of Persuasion" from the *Journal of Consumer Research*, demonstrated that the small act of remembering someone's name is perceived as a compliment, and increases their compliance in making a purchase.

Hoover Adams, founder of *The Daily Dunn*, would be the first person to agree with this. His local newspaper in Dunn, North Carolina, is one of the most successful newspapers in the country. On average, every household buys 1.12 copies, meaning every citizen in town has a subscription.

When asked what his secret was, Adams said his forty-year marketing strategy boiled down to three things: *Names, Names, and Names.* Adams discovered that what people wanted most out of a paper was to see their name, and their friends' names. Adams once said, "If I could, I'd publish pages from the phone book."

People love reading and hearing about themselves. One company has been nailing this strategy for years, while simultaneously making everyone else on the planet feel insecure about their lack of accomplishments: The *Forbes* "30 Under 30".

Every year *Forbes* randomly picks bright emerging stars from various fields, to feature as poster children for what we all could accomplish if we just stopped sharing cat videos on YouTube for twenty minutes.

I don't know about you, but you can bet if I was listed in the *Forbes* Top-Anything list, I would plop down and humble-brag that information all over my social media accounts. With every list, *Forbes* immediately leverages the social networks of the highly influential nominees who are primed to share their success with everyone they know. Genius!

Leveraging influencers is an integral part of social sharing and building online communities. The simplest way to put this strategy into practice immediately is to scout and blog a list of the top ten influencers, podcasts, books, or blogs in your industry one by one. Tweet an article link with each influencer's Twitter handle, and watch them quickly re-tweet and share it to their large online communities.

Influencer Priming:

Have you ever had a famous person share or respond to one of your tweets? It's thrilling.

If you want to get some major players involved in sharing your stuff, investigate who has a stake in your content. If you experience viral success, who are people and companies that would get a piece of the action? These people can help you.

For example, Michelle Phan's makeup tutorial references both Lady Gaga and several makeup lines and products. She would want to alert these stakeholders by blasting out an email or tweet to Lady GaGa's publicity team and L'Oreal to give them a heads up their products are being featured.

This is an excellent excuse to reach out and share your content with people, especially influencers with large online communities. The cool thing about the world we live in today is that you can reach these big names with a simple tweet or a well-crafted email.

Action Steps:

1. *Write a listicle or blog of high and medium influencers in your industry with engaged audiences or large followings, such as celebrities, podcasts, performers, TV shows, apps, bloggers, etc.

Influencers include stakeholders in the content itself. Although you may want to shoot for the A-List, emerging influencers and celebrities building their career can be more accessible and proactive.

**Be wary of direct competitors, although often teaming up with the competition can mean more success for everyone.*

2. Add emails or twitter handles of everyone mentioned to your list and remember to tag them or reach out to them directly when your content goes live. Share it with your networks and the selected list of influencers.

Chapter 13:

The Power of Ego Marketing

According to Freud, the ego is what balances our Id (dark, animalistic desires like sex and murder) and the superego (our need to be an upstanding citizen doing the right thing).

Our ego is mostly a constructed self-definition that we begin creating almost the day we are born. Humans become very involved and attached to the beliefs they have about what makes them unique and what makes them a part of certain groups, even if these beliefs are false.

We also have something called a "schema," which is our mental structure of preconceived ideas. The schema is a framework we use to make sense of the world or a system of organizing and perceiving new information. Once something has fit in our schema, it is difficult to get it out.

What does this Psych 101 crash course have to do with viral marketing? Everything. Almost every decision we make to share something online or purchase something is motivated by an innate desire, quest for approval, or need to reaffirm our unique identity.

Perhaps you live in Portland. Perhaps you own a pet or are the oldest in your family. All of these various factors determine who you are and how to identify in relation to the world and other groups.

Our schemas and experiences are all very different based on our gender, generation, age, political views, and other various social factors. However, thanks to this schema, you inevitably identify with certain groups of people.

Target Persona

To appeal to your audience's ego you have to know a little (or a lot) about their schema. The first step to this is to envision a person (or persona) who you are trying to appeal to.

Where do they live? What do they love? What are their hopes, dreams, and fears? Write down everything you can think up about them, from age to eating habits.

When it comes time to writing anything from ad campaigns to subject lines, this exercise will ensure you are speaking directly to your audience in a personalized way, instead of boring them with things they don't find interesting.

Let's say you live in Japan and you're perusing the Internet. Which post below is going to strike your interest more? Which are you more likely to share with your friends and communities?

"GIANT TIDAL WAVE HITTING CANADA TOMORROW"

"GIANT TIDAL WAVE HITTING JAPAN TOMORROW"

Yep, you're going to share the article about Japan getting desecrated and then buy some flood insurance. Here's another test. Let's say you own a miniature Schnauzer. Which ad is going appeal to you more?

Ad: "Dogs LOVE our doggy treats!"

You: I am not a dog. Who cares?

Ad: "People with dogs LOVE our doggy treats!"

You: That is weird that people love to eat doggy treats. But I'm a person and I have a dog, so, okay. Maybe they're referring people like me.

Ad: "San Francisco locals who own Miniature Schnauzers LOVE our doggy treats!"

You: I live in the Bay and own a miniature Schnauzer. Are they talking about me? COOL! If people just like me like this stuff, I bet I will too!

People love reading about the people and things they know and identify with. There is evidence of this in every Buzzfeed quiz. Titles such as, “What does your facial hair say about you?” or “10 ways you know you’re from Chicago” are popular and shared for a reason.

People feel special when they see something that represents them, which motivates them to share it.

Action Steps:

1. Craft your target persona. Who are they? Where do they live? What do they love?

2. Experiment writing hooks, headlines, ads, and content that directly reference elements of your target audience’s lifestyle.

Chapter 14:

Just Be Cool

A very large segment of social media addicts share content with others for one reason alone: it makes them look good. Sharing content is almost the digital equivalent of picking out an accessory or hairstyle for a day. Each post is a small element in the careful crafting of a public persona.

It's not rocket science. Social media power users want to share something that represents themselves or their friends in a funny, cool, or interesting way. When you see someone announce she is heading to Mexico for a beach vacation, chances are she wants her friends to think, "Wow! What a fascinating James Bond life of adventure and intrigue."

Fifteen years ago, if someone ate ice cream at Pinkberry there was little chance their friends and networks would ever know or care.

In today's digital world, everything is game for public news. People constantly choose whether or not to associate themselves with your product in full view of their friends and networks.

A social media advocate is allowing your business into their personal life and integrating your content as part of their digital identity. Your viral pieces should enhance someone's public persona, rather than detract.

Consider the delicacy of this relationship and how your media pieces and copy writing will make someone who shares look by association.

If you publish social media that inspires and delights, your audience will gladly engage with your brand to score social capital among their peers.

What IS cool?

Thousands of years ago Old English speakers used the root word *col* to refer to "unperturbed, undemonstrative". By definition, "cool" refers to a mild temperature, and in slang terms, a mild temperament.

Several investigations into our perception of "cool" have uncovered that it has something to do with social desirability, attractiveness, and success. But there is a certain "je ne sais quoi" to being cool many of us just can't put our finger on.

Being cool is the ability to keep your wits about you without allowing people and circumstances to impact that. It is the ability to just be you and own it. Hard.

Don't Try to Please Everyone All the Time.

Today, Facebook is a utility. The site never would have succeeded so far, so fast if it wasn't for the original niche of college students who shared the app as an inside club with all of their friends. Facebook quickly lost its 'insider only' status when it opened to the public and embraced total world domination.

While confidence is the key to cool, needing or begging for approval from others is death to cool.

The new kid on the social media block, SnapChat, is an app designed to be intentionally difficult to use. Tweens and college kids *love* this app because, one, their parents can't figure out how to use it to spy on them, and two, SnapChat is not trying to sycophant to every single audience on earth. SnapChat is appealing to a younger audience, not redesigning their app so everyone can use it.

Creating an inside joke or club, appeals to our sense of scarcity. As humans, if we sense availability to a resource is scarce (gas, tulips, gold, food, or social acceptance); it causes us to desire it more. Creating limited availability can trigger this pack survival instinct.

Stay current.

Fans and early-adopters want to be innovators of your product. Updating frequently and ensuring your communities are the first to know about cutting edge announcements will keep people checking back for more.

Don't be old news. Social media is a story that unfolds in real time. Internet users are obsessed with the new and aren't interested in association with pages and posts that appear distasteful or untrustworthy.

Listen.

People love to offer opinions and feel they're being heard. Asking questions will cause users to create a dialogue. The more user activity that occurs on your posts, the more you will be featured in feed stories and seen.

To create a sense of community and interesting conversation, encourage fans to participate with your memes. This can involve adding their creative spin, offering feedback, or participating in a quiz.

Own It.

At the startup conference Hustle Con 2016 in San Francisco, two heavy-hitters in the men's apparel scene, George Zimmer of Men's Warehouse, and Tom Montgomery of Chubbies Shorts, spoke about how they built brands around the concept of "cool". While each of these men possesses super coolness (successful, attractive, popular) and have created a brand to reflect this image, which won the 'Baby-Boomer verses Millennial' cool-factor contest on stage?

Before the two gentlemen began their discussion, a commercial was played as homage to the Chubbies shorts "brandgasm" the founders have infamously built into their social media and email marketing strategy. The video featured an overweight biker (Chubbies mascot and quintessential buyer persona) being fawned over by a thin, attractive female model wearing mostly nothing.

Classic 90's advertising with a modern-day hipster spin: the super-model eating a cheeseburger on a Ferrari, but aimed at a millennial demographic.

During their illuminating and educational conversation, Zimmer provided insights into how he built Men's Warehouse into a multi-million dollar empire: "We never used sexuality or scantily clad women, as other clothing stores did to sell merchandise. We tried to make it about facts and value. The baby boomers pride themselves on a surplus of reason and a shortage of emotion." To soften the blow, he followed his statement with, "Your generation understands it doesn't have to be an either/or situation."

The audience tweets went wild, and women in the audience loved this statement (for obvious reasons). The clincher and subtext was that Men's Wearhouse didn't need to rely on sexy women, cheeseburgers, or Ferraris to sell a product, or to be cool. Their product stood on it's own for any reasonable person to see.

If you are looking to apply confidence to your brand, the worst thing you can do is shout '50% Off Sale' from the rooftops and plaster discounts all over your social media pieces. Cheap gimmicks or slashing your prices screams insecurity and desperation, and customers can sense it.

While the occasional discount or hard sell on social media is acceptable for your 'Insider's Club', it is often akin to asking for sex on the first date and can be a turn off.

A confident brand utilizing social media to provide value and build lasting relationships will garner respect and loyalty, attract better customers, and result in lucrative business results. Treat your digital audiences with respect, and they will return the favor.

Action Steps:

- Own your look. Either be aesthetically pleasing, or if you are going to have an ugly website, make sure it is intentional.
- Appeal to sub-cultures instead of trying to please everyone, all the time.
- Create an inside joke or club for people who "get it".
- Avoid desperation and gimmicks. Focus on creating and providing value, before requesting something in return.

Chapter 15:

Sharing is Caring – Tit for Tat & The Rule of Reciprocity

In today's distraction-filled and complex world, our limited attention spans only seem to be getting shorter. If you are coming up short on ideas, why not try this daring yet effective approach: capture the attention of your audience by making their life better.

It is a simple and life-affirming concept: a wonderful way to break through Internet clutter is to help people by providing them with value, plain and simple.

Humans tend to be a little self-involved, especially when they want something. Many businesses and brands can get caught up in what they want. It is easy to fall in love with the details of your product, or become so focused on the next sale, that you forget why you are in business in the first place: to enhance the lives of others.

The Reciprocity Effect

It has become well known in the world of psychology that people are inclined to give back what they have received. This is why master seducers always know to pick up the tab on the first date. They are aware that people are more likely to say yes to those who they owe.

Have any of these scenarios played out in your life? A pal invites you to their party, and you feel obligated to invite them to your next bash. Your neighbor dog sits, causing you to want to water their plant next time she leaves town.

It is theorized that this 'tit for tat' behavioral custom is a result of evolution. Our instinct to return favors is thought to be a biological predisposition to our dependence on one another for survival. Free loading cavemen were most likely ex-communicated from their tribe, meaning the more socially savvy of us survived and thrived long enough to pass the trait of generosity to offspring.

Even rats understand the principle of generosity. Researchers found rats not only offer help to those that have helped them before, but the quality of help provided is adjusted according to the perceived value of what they will get in return. The 'tit-for-tat' behavioral patterns are seen again and again throughout the animal kingdom.

The principle of reciprocity is a crucial one to understand in business, as Robert Cialdini illustrates in this scenario of how a waiter can use favors to increase tip amounts:

"So the last time you visited a restaurant, there's a good chance that the waiter or waitress will have given you a gift. Probably about the same time that they bring your bill. A liqueur, perhaps, or a fortune cookie, or perhaps a simple mint.

So here's the question. Does the giving of a mint have any influence over how much tip you're going to leave them? Most people will say no. But that mint can make a surprising difference. In the study, giving diners a single mint at the end of their meal typically increased tips by around 3%.

If the gift is doubled and two mints are provided, tips don't double. They quadruple—a 14% increase in tips. But perhaps most interesting of all is the fact that if the waiter provides one mint, starts to walk away from the table, but pauses, turns back and says, 'For you nice people, here's an extra mint,' tips go through the roof. A 23% increase, influenced not by what was given, but how it was given."

Keeping this in mind will keep your social media and digital presence from getting needy. Here is an example of needy copywriting, as compared to cultivating an air of useful confidence:

PLEASE like my Facebook page!

Subtext: I really need help and I need you to like me. Please?

Verses:

Follow my Facebook page, and I will send you special discounts!

Subtext: I can help you save money so you can spend it on something else you love, like doughnuts.

Special deals perform exceptionally well because they are the most distilled form of offering value: free money.

This applies even more so to emotional posts, humor, and storytelling. A video about a cat falling off a couch will make you laugh and brighten your day. A makeup video tutorial can help you pull off a super cool Halloween costume to impress your friends. An article about a single mom defying the odds to build a successful business will offer you inspiration and an emotional catharsis.

Providing value invokes people to share your content. You don't have to perfect a comedic routine or unveil a new scientific discovery to provide valuable knowledge to others. Sometimes generating excellent and useful content is as a simple as being the person who is willing to research and document a learning experience.

"How-To" videos and posts perform exceptionally well because people like to share beneficial information with others. Unlike news or gossip with an expiration date, educational content is "evergreen", meaning it will continue to be relevant and referred to long after it's publish date, appreciating value over time.

What Do I Have To Say That Hasn't Already Been Said?

If you think creating useful content is difficult, think again. You are a lifetime of interesting knowledge and experiences, even if you take your skills for granted.

Half of the battle of creating useful content is compilation. There are novices in every field that need the basics to be easily accessible. Teaching as you learn can also be surprisingly effective, as you will better understand your audience's beginning vantage point.

A friend of mine discovered this when she started learning to code, and in the process took notes and blogged everything she learned. I recall thinking the exercises she wrote about were so simple. I looked at them and thought, "I could have written that in my sleep!" However, as an advanced coder, I was making the mistake of taking my knowledge for granted.

What is the difference between my friend and I? She wrote the information down and I didn't. Beginners who knew nothing about coding started to refer to her website to gather basics and an easy introduction. As her knowledge progressed, so did the advancement of her tutorials and the numbers of readership. Now whenever I have a friend who asks where to start when learning to code, I pull one of her blogs and send it to them, just because it is a simple, easy-to-use resource. Her website has taken off and she makes a full time living with her blog content and selling online coding courses.

Providing value also involves asking for feedback and listening to your customers. Social media is not the same a billboard advertisement on the side of a highway. Don't be that guy on Facebook who is awkwardly talking to himself, by himself in a crowded room. Make sure your conversations on social media are there to create a relationship and form a two-way dialogue.

Will I Give Away Trade Secrets?

That is up to you, but probably not. Mark Twain said it best:

"There is no such thing as a new idea. It is impossible. We simply take a lot of old ideas and put them into a sort of mental kaleidoscope. We give them a turn and they make new and curious combinations. We keep on turning and making new combinations indefinitely; but they are the same old pieces of colored glass that have been in use through all the ages."

Someone is reading your work because they are interested in your perspective on things, and will probably hire you or buy a product from you for the same reasons. You might as well contribute your "mental kaleidoscope" to the Internet ether.

Creating educational content has many benefits, including establishing thought leadership in the mind of your audience. This means you will be considered an expert and guide on their learning journey, and make them even more inclined to pay you for your knowledge and expertise in the future.

If nothing else, you'll gain some major karma points for helping and educating others.

Action Steps:

1. Think about questions you get asked a lot.

For example "How did you learn how to do a hand-stand? How do you keep your apartment so clean? How did you find your great job?" Write five to ten steps or tips on how to accomplish these things, and hit the publish button on your blog.

2. Research top search results or competitor blog posts on your topic. Use those headlines as writing prompts.

3. Think about something you have achieved and the path you took to get there. Break it down, step-by-step, in a blog.

4. Compile a list of top blogs, podcasts, books, or resources on a topic.

5. Most importantly, for something to be useful, it must be actionable. Make sure that your content gives audiences action steps they can apply to their own lives, now, today.

Chapter 16:

Algorithms – The Method Behind the Madness

In wake of the 2016 election, nothing became more evident to everyone that algorithms were ruling more than just the Internet. Computer algorithms have seeped into our daily lives, impacting the products we buy online, the politicians we vote for, and even the worldview we consume.

Facebook's wild profits are due to the automated process of algorithms. It discovers what users like, finds advertisers that want to hit those interests, marries the two and takes the money. No humans necessary.

For this reason, viral marketing is both an intuitive art and hard science that requires comprehension of human *and* computer behavior.

While this book is dedicated to primal human responses to stimuli, we must acknowledge that algorithms also now play a profound role in what lives and dies on the Internet. The good news is modern algorithms are designed to intuit popularity. Please humans first with something great, and computers will pick-up and follow.

Websites like Udemy, Etsy, and Instagram all have very different, but specific algorithms and user-experiences designed to ensure their websites are addicting and easy to use.

The art of being an Internet whisperer is often to discover what these algorithms are, and outsmart them. For example, many marketers are savvy to how algorithms are prone to popularity detection by tracking reviews, likes, clicks, or purchases.

Organic (unpaid) digital success is often a snowball effect. If an algorithm detects something is receiving an onslaught of attention, it raises the search result rank. The more successful something becomes, the more traction it gains.

Unfortunately, penning a book about the specific algorithms for each website could be a waste of time, because they are different for every website, and can change on the whim of a company or programmer.

Fortunately (as a general rule) algorithms are designed to detect what humans enjoy, and give them more of it. For example, if you enjoy purchasing chocolate on Amazon, Amazon will display many different types of chocolate for you. To get a head start on algorithms, make sure you give anything you publish on a running head start.

This doesn't mean participating in bizarre black-hat computer hacker scams. Instead, make sure to always share what you create with friends and family, and use tags and keywords whenever possible.

If the art and science of algorithms intrigues you, stay tuned for my next book on search engine optimization. Meanwhile, here are a few terms that you can familiarize yourself with to make sure you are ahead of the game with your digital presence.

Algorithm - A step-by-step procedure for solving a problem or accomplishing some end especially by a computer. This is how social media sites read and interpret what you share to determine how it will reach other users in a newsfeed or search result.

Search Engine Optimization (SEO) - Ensuring that your website appears high on the list of results returned by a search engine (such as Google) to maximize the number of visitors and website traffic.

User experience design (**UX**, **UXD**, **UED** or **XD**) - The art and science of measuring and improving the usability, accessibility, and pleasure in the interaction with a digital product or website.

Big Data- Extremely large data sets that may be analyzed computationally to reveal patterns, trends, and associations, especially relating to human behavior and interactions.

Chapter 17

BONUS: VIRAL QUIZ- Burning Man vs. Sandwiches

Now that you have learned the secret sauce to perfecting your digital body language, it is time to put your skills to the test. This will probably be the most entertaining quiz you have ever taken in your life. All you have to do to pass is watch a wacky video.

If you don't already know, Burning Man is a weeklong art and hippie festival that takes place in the desert. Some people love Burning Man and will eat up any and all media surrounding it. Others are weary of all of the hype and are certain it's just a bunch of hippies and tech billionaires looking for an excuse to do drugs in the desert.

Needless to say, because “Burners” are such a fanatical bunch, the topic has become pretty divisive. Either way, poking fun of Burning Man is all the rage on the Internet right now.

Whatever your personal stance, we can all say for sure that Burning Man has absolutely nothing to do with Quizno’s sandwiches. But this didn’t stop the sandwich company from taking full advantage of a prime viral opportunity, releasing the video “Burn Trials - Out of the Maze and onto the Playa.”

With 2.6 million views and counting, this video has stirred up waves upon waves of attention, and is an impeccable combination of every viral element, making it perfect material for you to test the new theories you have learned.

As a final exercise to get you thinking, let’s dissect the strategy behind why this video went insanely viral, spawning press, controversy, and exposure for the Quizno’s brand.

If you are ready to test your knowledge, watch the video for yourself and try to identify and make a list of how many viral elements you can find at play.

Go ahead. I'll wait. Here is the link if you need it:

http://www.annalisc.com/**viral-resources/**

Did you watch it? Now check the list below to examine how the video utilized the viral devices you have learned.

- Hooks
- Story-Telling
- Faces
- Eyes
- Emotion
- Awe
- Surprise
- Movement
- Sub-cultures
- Influencers
- Satire
- 'Cool'
- Ego Marketing
- Controversial
- Useful

First and foremost, the ad brilliantly implements the power of storytelling with classic Hollywood techniques. Our characters are embarking upon a personal quest of self-discovery, only to find themselves trapped in a strange backward universe of anti-consumerism.

Because the chosen format for this satire is video, faces, characters, and movement are integral to the format. A festival setting like Burning Man offers extravagant buffet of visual delights.

The video quickly keys into the vital tool of emotion, beginning with awe and leading into humor and surprise. The experience of Burning Man is something that has inspired so many, and the video depicts the *awe* encapsulated in the event's strange, over-the-top art structures and activities.

The video attempts to be useful but fumbles, flashing a Quizno's Sandwich coupon across the screen so quickly, it almost seems like an attempt at subliminal messaging. Most likely this is because the video's creators understood that any longer that a fraction of a second could constitute as an over-sell.

The viral video also spoofs Burning Man with a post-apocalyptic, sci-fi undertone and unapologetically mocks festival goers, Burners, hippies, the Maze Runner series, and especially its target market: millennials.

The video blatantly teases its target demographic causing them to think, "That is *so* me!" Because it is relatable to millennials, festivalgoers, or anyone who has attended Burning Man, it *incentivizes* target niches to share and incorporate it into their online identities.

The main characters are portrayed as keeping their "cool" in a foreign land of fanatical, die-hard Instagram wannabes.
The video then takes a risk, tapping into the emotion of rage by tight roping between the divisive groups of who those love Burning Man, and those who love to hate Burning Man. Many Burners were outraged by the blatant product placement, which caused them to *share* it in protest.

Adding gasoline to the viral fire, Burning Man responded to this video's use of its brand by threatening a lawsuit. A media circus ensued, and the video received more hits as debate and controversy erupted over whether or not it was appropriate for Burning Man to sue for the misrepresentation of its brand.

Whatever the production costs of this video, you can't buy that kind of media attention. I guarantee it costs a lot less to make a funny film in the desert than spend thousands on media buying and pay-per-click campaigns.

CONCLUSION

> "Progress is impossible without change, and those who cannot change their minds cannot change anything." George Bernard Shaw

Similarly the way television was criticized for being a "trend", social media endures a lot of criticism from luddites and computer geniuses alike. Some critics believe that the Internet information age is degrading personal communication and diminishing face-to-face interaction. On the other end of the spectrum, technology savants sometimes view social media as an overly simplified definition of Internet culture with no real palpable value.

To those who believe social media is easy for anyone to do and constitutes as a phony Web 2.0 trend with hacks and spammers, perhaps it is only because their gift of technology prowess has come so easily to them. It is premature to criticize a structure still nascent in its development.

These critics do not see the world I see. A world in which social media provides the opportunity to form friendships, keep in touch, pioneer groups, contact heroes, land jobs, rally for causes, and cultivate hundreds of profound personal relationships via binary code.

Thanks to the Internet, human connections are placed at your fingertips and once insurmountable goals can now be accomplished through the click of a button.

Why only use this profound super power to stalk your long-lost ex or compare yourselves to your friends, when you can use it to persuade, entertain, or achieve world domination?

Does social media and online culture improve the human experience or detract from it? You make the choice.

In my career of ten years, I've found that when done correctly, social media and viral content can be the most lucrative investment you can make in your business or personal brand, above paid advertising and other methods.

In case you were wondering what happened to our viral stars, Double Rainbow Guy and makeup artist Michelle Phan took exceedingly different paths. Like a bad VH1 *Behind the Music* special, Vasquez tried to recreate his Double Rainbow moment by posting a thousand videos of him in nature talking. It fell flat and he became a one-hit wonder.

In comparison, Michelle parlayed her video fame into a production company and a multi-million dollar business. Phan is the second-most-watched female YouTuber in the world, with nearly seven million subscribers, amassing over one billion views. Thanks to her makeup tutorials, Phan became the official video makeup artist for Lancôme and has created her own line for L'Oreal.

So why did these two stars take such different paths?
Some would say it comes down to hard work, and providing value.

Phan spent years tirelessly cultivating a YouTube channel by crafting and honing the art of valuable, useful content for her audience. When people saw her video of the Lady Gaga eyes, they discovered her other fifty high-quality videos that were unrecognized until her viral moment.

Her diligence and dedication enabled her to win over fans and achieve momentum to surmount becoming just a one-hit wonder. The lesson is this: social media is a slow burn that appreciates value over time. Content marketing is both fleeting and eternal. To sell more of your product, create meaningful relationships with customers and increase awareness, you must creatively promote your brand and think long term.

Blog posts and social media pages can live on in infamy but only when they evolve and reinvent. The more you put in the leg work and stay on top of the learning curve, the more valuable your return and results will be.

Who knows? Maybe you'll get lucky and go viral tomorrow. But when that happens, do you have what it takes to keep your audience coming back for more? Investing in your digital brand presence will ensure that when you strike a viral match, you have the gasoline to fuel a long-burning fire.

To your viral success,

Annalis Clint

Digital Behavior Specialist & Content Marketing Coach
AnnalisC.com

PS- If you enjoyed this book, please don't be shy to drop me a line, leave a review, or both. I love reading feedback and reviews are the lifeblood of Kindle books, so they are always welcome and greatly appreciated.

SPEAKING AND COACHING:

Imagine going far beyond the contents of this book and dramatically improving the way you interact with the world, and manifesting successful real life results and relationships from simple digital interactions.

Are you interested in contacting Annalis? She is available for:

- A social media workshop for your work place
- Speaking engagements on the power of digital body language
- Personalized UX research and digital brand coaching
- And so much more

Annalis speaks around the world to help people improve their lives through the power of building relationships, content strategy, and creating successful real life results through digital communication.

Annalis is a recognized industry expert, best-selling author, and speaker. To invite Annalis to speak at your next event, or to inquire about coaching, get in touch directly through her website's contact at www.annalisc.com or email at socialstruck@gmail.com.

CHEAT SHEET:

1. Your Fifteen Minutes

Customer behavior and spending dollars are migrating online fast. Social platforms empower you to broadcast your life, image, and business or product, to an unfathomably large audience. More importantly, digital promotion allows you to empower a niche of loyal and dedicated followers to your brand or persona.

2. The Secret Behind Overnight Success

The key to making your 'meme' (shareable content piece) go viral is to leverage personalization and subcultures. As in any industry, the secret behind overnight success is hard work. Creating viral content calls upon a breadth of resources, skills and talents, and is filled with trial and error experimentation.

3. These 19 Headline Formulas Will Make Your Content Unstoppable

Create an open loop or hook headline to help stick in your audience's long-term memory. Use analogies, numbers, and anticipation to standout in a news feed. Create a set-up (question, fragment sentence, or intriguing scenario) to prepare the reader, and excite them for what is to come.

4. Memory Tricks and the 'Information Smoothie'

Use numbers, categories, chunking, special organization, the Serial Position effect, and special formatting to encourage reading, sharing, and digestion of your message.

5. The Secret to Telling a $^%*@# Fantastic Story

Narratives and stories capture your audience's brain and allow it to sync up with your own. Use elements including protagonists, desire, conflict, and resolution to make your message exciting and compelling.

6. Three Viral Emotions that Get Shared the Most

Use emotion to draw your audience in. Rage, awe, and surprise are the emotions that get shared the most online. Harness these emotions by delivering the unexpected, creating an inside joke, or pitting two groups against each other.

7. Show Instead of Tell: The Picture Superiority Effect

Two-thirds of your brain is dedicated to the functioning of your vision, which is why photos are easier to process and more powerful than words.

8. The Jennifer Aniston Neuron

We are attracted to recognizable faces, to the point that our brain will even create special 'neurons' for people we are familiar with. This explains the success of Facebook and celebrity gossip. Create and use familiar faces to associate with your brand.

9. Create an Unspoken Connection with THIS Trick, Used by Disney, Cereal Box Cartoons, and Italian Courtiers . . .

Use the power of eye contact and gaze to catch attention or direct a viewer's attention where you want it to go. Our pupils dilate to take in more of what we like, meaning larger-than-life pupils are sure to be a crowd-pleaser. Babies and cats blow up the Internet again and again because their large eyes and features trigger the innate, hard-wire nurturing instinct in our brain.

10. How Emojis Are Changing Our Brain ☺

Emojis now trigger the same response in the brain as human facial expressions. Facial expressions are another way to create a reaction in your audience because we tend to mimic and mirror expressions, which causes us to feel the emotion we are mimicking.

11. Mesmerizing with Motion

Our eyes are drawn to motion, which makes using videos and GIFs a magnetic draw for your viral pieces.

12. Names, Names, Names: Influencer Priming

People love reading about themselves, and are inclined to share things they have been mentioned in. To leverage influencers and build your online community, name or quote people directly in your content.

13. Ego Marketing

In an age of information clutter, people are inclined to tune in when information they see or hear pertains directly to them, or groups they identify with. Craft your target audience persona and ensure your hooks, headlines, ads, and content provide a benefit or reference to a niche.

14. Just Be Cool

Desperation and people pleasing can only get you so far. Cultivating confidence is just as important in digital body language as it is in real life. Appealing to sub-cultures or inside influencers will ensure everyone else will want to follow.

15. Tit for Tat & The Rule of Reciprocity: Why Sharing is Caring

Creating value ignites a relationship with your customers and audience, which creates a symbiotic exchange and builds trust. Instead of asking for you want, give something first. One of the easiest ways to give your audience a valuable gift is through the exchange of information. Offering educational content has many benefits, including establishing thought leadership, and creating 'evergreen' content to be shared again and again.

16. Algorithms- The Method Behind the Madness

Despite the underlying psychology of what people love to share and engage with online, there are always unseen factors that determine what rises to the top. Every website from Facebook to Etsy has an 'black box' algorithm that determines what products or posts are shown, and these algorithms change frequently. The more an algorithm interprets something as popular (through likes, reviews, clicks, favorites, and more), the more visible it will become.

Conclusion- Whether you believe that social media is a ridiculous trend or a revolution here to stay, there is no arguing that investment in your online presence for your personal and professional life can reap massive rewards, when done correctly.

Selected Bibliography and Citations

- Shane Snow, *Smartcuts, How Hackers, Innovators and Icons Accelerate Success,* HarperBusiness, 2014.
- Jonah Berger, *Contagious: Why Things Catch On*, Simon and Schuster, 2013.
- Robert Cialdini, *Influence*, Harper Business; Revised edition, 2006
- Malcolm Gladwell, *The Tipping Point*, Back Bay Books, 2002
- Bluma Zeigarnik, *On finished and unfinished tasks. A source book of Gestalt psychology*, 1, 1-15 (1938).
- Annie Murphy Paul, *Your Brain on Fiction*, (The *New York Times*, 2012).
- Ryan Holiday, *Trust Me, I'm Lying,* Portfolio, 2012.
- Marcus Woo, *Single-Cell Recognition: A Halle Berry Brain Cell*, (California Institute of Technology, 2005).
- R. Buck, *Nonverbal behavior and the theory of emotion: The facial feedback hypothesis"*, (Journal of Personality and Social Psychology, 1980).
- Daniel J. Howard, Charles Gengler and Ambuj Jain, *What's in a Name? A Complementary Means of Persuasion,* (Journal of Consumer Research, 1995, Vol. 22)
- Vanessa Van Edwards, "10 Ways Body Language is Used in Advertising", last modified March 10, 2017, http://www.scienceofpeople.com/2013/08/5-ways-body-language-is-used-in-advertising/
- Katherine Baildon, summary of Musicus, Aviva, Aner Tal, and Brian Wansink (2014). Eyes in the Aisles: Why is Cap'n Crunch Looking Down at My Child? *Environment & Behavior, 47(7), 715-733.* doi: 10.1177/0013916514528793, http://foodpsychology.cornell.edu/discoveries/cereal-box-psychology
- Sam Parr, "Step by Step for Viral Content: Going from 0 to 250K Views", July 2014, http://www.growhack.com/2014/07/step-by-step-for-creating-viral-content-going-to-250k-views/
- Andrew Tate, "10 Scientific Reasons People are Wired to Respond to Your Visual Marketing", May 19, 2015, https://designschool.canva.com/blog/visual-marketing/

- Jerry Corley, "What's the Key to a Good Joke?", April 21, 2011, http://www.standupcomedyclinic.com/whats-the-key-to-a-good-joke/
- Hannah Osborne, "Rats remember their friends in tit-for-tat behavior" February 27, 2015, http://www.ibtimes.co.uk/rats-remember-their-friends-tit-tat-behaviour-1489820
- Roger Kay, "Generous Tit For Tat: A Winning Strategy" December 19, 2011, https://www.forbes.com/sites/rogerkay/2011/12/19/generous-tit-for-tat-a-winning-strategy/ - 6723229866eb

Printed in Great Britain
by Amazon